First Edition Collectible

A Genuine Autographed Manuscript of Sharon Esther Lampert

Every Thought In Your Head Was Put There By A Writer

Sharon Esther Lampert
Poet, Prophet, Philosopher, Paladin of Education, Pinup, Prodigy

Date:

To:

From:

Message:

All of humanity's problems stem from man's inability to sit quietly in a room alone.

Blaise Pascal
French Philosopher

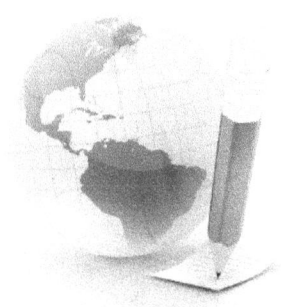

WRITERS RUN THE WORLD

10 Secrets For Spinning Good Ideas Into Great Ideas

A Writer's Pocket Notebook
Professional & Personal Life Planner
The 7-Shifts Schedule

Self-Help, English, Writing, Journalism
WRITERS RUN THE WORLD
10 Secrets For Spinning Good Ideas Into Great Ideas
A Writer's Pocket Notebook
Professional & Personal Life Planner
The 7-Shifts Schedule

©2022 by Sharon Esther Lampert. All Rights Reserved.
No part of this book may be used or reproduced in any manner whatsoever without written permission except in the case of brief quotations embodied in critical articles and reviews.

Dedication

MOMMY
Love of My Lifetime

Palm Beach Book Publisher Books may be purchased for education, business or sales promotional use.

Palm Beach Book Publisher
Full Service Publisher: Write, Edit, Publish, Market, Sales
www.PalmBeachBookPublisher.com
Phone: 917-767-5843

ISBN Paperback: 978-1-885872-84-5
Library of Congress Catalog Card Number: 2021902701

Author Website and Fan Mail:
www.WritersRuntheWorld.com
FANS@WritersRuntheWorld.com
FANS@SharonEstherLampert.com

Book Design and Interior: Creatve Genius Sharon Esther Lampert

Editor: Dave Segal

Global Online Orders and Distribution:
INGRAM 1 Ingram Blvd. La Vergne, TN 37086-3629
Phone: 615-793-5000, Fax orders: 615-287-6990

First Edition
Manufactured in the United States of America

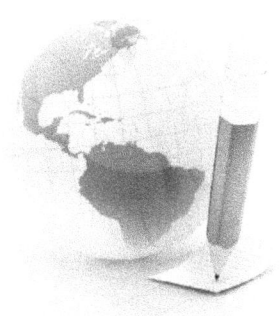

WRITERS RUN THE WORLD

10 Secrets For Spinning Good Ideas Into Great Ideas

A Writer's Pocket Notebook

Professional & Personal Life Planner
The 7-Shifts Schedule

Palm Beach Book Publisher
BOOKS ARE POWERFUL!
EDUCATE! ENLIGHTEN! EMPOWER!
ENTERTAIN! EMANCIPATE! EVOLUTION!

What Do Books Do?
BOOKS ARE POWERFUL!
Books Educate!
Books Enlighten!
Books Empower!
Books Entertain!
Books Emancipate!
Books Spring Eternal!
Books Drive Exploration!
Books Spark Evolution!
Books Ignite Revolution!

Philosopher-Queen-Prodigy Sharon Esther Lampert

Table of Contents

Introduction
Good, Great, and Gifted Writers
1-3

Professional & Personal Life Planner & The 7-Shifts Schedule
4-5

Table of Contents
10 Secrets For Spinning Good Ideas Into Great Ideas
6-7

A Writer's Pocket Notebook
9-59

APPENDIX
10 Secrets For Spinning Good Ideas Into Great Ideas
61-75

About Creative Genius Sharon Esther Lampert
90-91

WRITERS RUN THE WORLD

The space can be humble, probably should be ... and it really needs only one thing: a door which you are willing to shut!
– Stephen King

10 Secrets For Spinning Good Ideas Into Great Ideas

Introduction

Good, Great, and Gifted Writers

Not only do you need to learn to write as a writer writes, but to think as a writer thinks.

Every writer writes the exact same way—one word at a time!

Every writer starts with a blank piece of paper—and transforms nothing into something!

First, every writer uses the lateral-thinking right brain to create; and second, uses the linear-thinking left brain to proofread for errors. The linear thinking left brain can be taught and trained to proofread to perfection. The creative lateral right brain is an inherited innate gift. In 1967, these distinctions were first coined by Edward de Bono.

Most writers look forward to the day, when just like a catepiller that undergoes transformation into a butterfly—an aspiring writer will transform into a published author!

Writing is an art form similar to drawing, painting, sculpting and singing—you can teach someone the mechanics of writing, but not the **ART** of writing. Every writer has a distinct form of expression, and unique fingerprint and signature. In comparison to singing, each singer has an inborn voice, and this voice can be trained to play scales and sing songs with well-crafted arrangements, but each singer's genetic inherited voice will alter the expression of the song—and singers like writers can be divided into three distinct groups: **Good, Great,** and **Gifted**!

Before you sit down to write, ask yourself these questions:

1. Where do I write?
2. When do I write?
3. How long should I write at any one time?
4. How do I write? Fiction or Non-Fiction? Research or Imagination?
5. What is the process? (Numerous Rough Drafts to a Final Draft)
6. What other items will I need to be able to write? Coffee or Tea?
7. Are you an early bird or a night owl?

WRITERS RUN THE WORLD

A Writer's Lifestyle: Write, Drink & Pee!

1. Room with No Distractions ✓
2. Spacious Writer's Desk ✓
3. Comfortable Chair ✓
4. Great Lighting ✓
5. Nearby Bathroom Breaks: "Write, Drink & Pee!" ✓
6. Exercise Breaks: Get Up & Stretch Every Hour (use weights) ✓
7. Energy Bites: Writing Takes Enormous Energy ✓
    a. Art of 10-Minute Meals: broccoli & crumbled goat cheese
    b. Healthy Snacks: celery sticks & humus, apples & almond butter
    c. Hydration: sugar-free water (add: lemon, honey & ginger)
    d. Avoid toxic processed, junk & fast foods (empty calories)
    e. Avoid addictive foods with sugar & salt (eliminate cravings)
8. Background Classical Music Recommendation
    Mendelsohn: E Minor, Op.64, Allegro Molto Appassionato
9. Sleep Routine (afternoon naps rejuvenate) ✓

Writing Instruments & Digital Tools

1. Pens and Pencils ✓
2. Pocket Notebook for Good & Great Ideas, pp. 9-59 ✓
3. Planner to Organize Professional & Personal Life, p. 4 ✓
4. Shift Schedule to Organize Professional & Personal Life, p. 5 ✓
5. Personal Computer: APPLE Mac ✓
6. Writing Software: Microsoft Word & Textedit Speech Software ✓
7. External Back-Ups: External Drive & USB Pen Drive ✓
8. Printer & Ink ✓
9. HUB for Computer, External Hard Drives, Printer, Cell Phone & Apple Watch, and Coffeemaker ✓

10 Secrets For Spinning Good Ideas Into Great Ideas

What Are a Writer's Distractions?
EVERYTHING!
Limit Flexible Repetitive Chores

Fixed Daily Biological Activities

1. Fixed: Eating - 3X Daily
2. Fixed: Bathroom - 3X Daily
3. Fixed: Sleep - 8 Hours

Flexible Weekly Chores

1. Flexible Chore: Groceries — Buy frozen food for zero waste
2. Flexible Chore: Meals — Prepare 5-10 minute meals
3. Flexible Chore: Frozen Food — Freezer food is safe for months!
4. Flexible Chore: Mail — Process personal mail once a week
5. Flexible Chore: Phone — Answer social phone calls: 7 p.m.- 9 p.m.

Flexible Monthly Chores

1. Flexible Chore: Bill Pay (1X Month)
   Call credit card companies, and ask them to change payment dates to same day of the month. Pay all bills once a month on exact same date.

2. Flexible Chore: Laundry (1X Month)
   Buy 30 DAYS worth of underwear, socks and bathroom towels

3. Flexible Chore: Household Chores (2X Month)
   DIY or delegate to a professional. Chasing dust around a room is one of the absurdities in life. Give away the dust collectors!

4. 1st of Month: Laundry, Back Up Computer, Clean Apt & Pay Bills

WRITERS RUN THE WORLD

Date: _____

1. DO DOING DONE
2. DIY or Delegate?
3. Distractions? Detours? Delays?

Professional Life

Urgent:
_____
_____
_____
_____
_____

Important:
_____
_____
_____
_____
_____
_____
_____
_____
_____
_____
_____

Low:
_____
_____
_____
_____

Work Stress Level: ____ (1-10)
Home Stress Level: ____ (1-10)

Personal Life

Practice Daily Gratitude
I am grateful for: _____

Practice Positive Self-Talk
"Please Don't Let Me Die with a Typo!"

Daily Healthy Food Choices:
Breakfast: _____
Lunch: _____
Dinner: _____

Exercise: Stretch, Walk, Gym, Sports (move!)
_____

Daily Expenses:
Spend: $ _____
Save: $ _____
Splurge: $ _____

Family/Friends/Neighbors/Strangers/Pets:
_____

Errands:
_____

Grocery:
_____

Household Chores:
_____

FREE Time—ME Time:
Read Book: _____
TV/Movie: _____
Nightlife: _____
Travel: _____

@2021. All Rights Reserved. WritersRunTheWorld.com

10 Secrets For Spinning Good Ideas Into Great Ideas

The 7-Shifts Schedule

Early Bird Shift 1. 5-8 a.m.

Shift 2. 9 a.m.-Noon

Shift 3. Noon-3 p.m.

Shift 4. 3p.m.-6 p.m.

Shift 5. 6 p.m.-9 p.m.

Shift 6. 9 p.m.-12 p.m.

Night Owl Shift 7. 12 a.m.-3 a.m.

WRITERS RUN THE WORLD

10 Secrets
For Spinning Good Ideas Into Great Ideas

Writers Are Artists Who Paint with Words

Sharon Esther Lampert

How Many Fingers Does a Writer Have? 11

Sharon Esther Lampert

10 Secrets For Spinning Good Ideas Into Great Ideas

#1 Writer's Toolbox
BRAINSTORM FOR GREAT IDEAS
63

#2 Writer's Toolbox
ASK GREAT QUESTIONS
65

#3 Writer's Toolbox
TAKE GREAT NOTES
67

#4 Writer's Toolbox
GREAT OUTLINES AND ORGANIZATION
71

#5 Writer's Toolbox
GREAT RESEARCH: PRIMARY SOURCES
73

#6 Writer's Toolbox
GREAT CRITICAL THINKING TACTICS
75

#7 Writer's Toolbox
10 ESOTERIC LAWS OF GENIUS AND CREATIVITY BY PRODIGY SHARON ESTHER LAMPERT
77

#8 Writer's Toolbox
READ GREAT WRITERS
79

#9 Writer's Toolbox
PROOFREADING TO PERFECTION
85

#10 Writer's Toolbox
FEEDBACK: FRESH EYES
87

WRITERS RUN THE WORLD

LITERATURE IS POWERFUL BEYOND WORDS FOR IT CREATES WORLDS

Sharon Esther Lampert
Poet, Philosopher, Prophet, Peacemaker & Prodigy

10 Secrets For Spinning Good Ideas Into Great Ideas

"It is perfectly okay to write garbage—
as long as you edit brilliantly."
—C.J. Cherryh

A Writer's Pocket Notebook

10 Secrets For Spinning Good Ideas Into Great Ideas

A Writer's Pocket Notebook

10 Secrets For Spinning Good Ideas Into Great Ideas

10 Secrets For Spinning Good Ideas Into Great Ideas

A Writer's Pocket Notebook

10 Secrets For Spinning Good Ideas Into Great Ideas

A Writer's Pocket Notebook

10 Secrets For Spinning Good Ideas Into Great Ideas

A Writer's Pocket Notebook

10 Secrets For Spinning Good Ideas Into Great Ideas

A Writer's Pocket Notebook

10 Secrets For Spinning Good Ideas Into Great Ideas

A Writer's Pocket Notebook

10 Secrets For Spinning Good Ideas Into Great Ideas

A Writer's Pocket Notebook

10 Secrets For Spinning Good Ideas Into Great Ideas

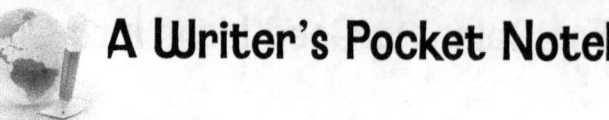

10 Secrets For Spinning Good Ideas Into Great Ideas

A Writer's Pocket Notebook

10 Secrets For Spinning Good Ideas Into Great Ideas

A Writer's Pocket Notebook

10 Secrets For Spinning Good Ideas Into Great Ideas

A Writer's Pocket Notebook

10 Secrets For Spinning Good Ideas Into Great Ideas

A Writer's Pocket Notebook

10 Secrets For Spinning Good Ideas Into Great Ideas

A Writer's Pocket Notebook

10 Secrets For Spinning Good Ideas Into Great Ideas

A Writer's Pocket Notebook

10 Secrets For Spinning Good Ideas Into Great Ideas

A Writer's Pocket Notebook

10 Secrets For Spinning Good Ideas Into Great Ideas

A Writer's Pocket Notebook

10 Secrets For Spinning Good Ideas Into Great Ideas

10 Secrets For Spinning Good Ideas Into Great Ideas

A Writer's Pocket Notebook

10 Secrets For Spinning Good Ideas Into Great Ideas

A Writer's Pocket Notebook

10 Secrets For Spinning Good Ideas Into Great Ideas

A Writer's Pocket Notebook

10 Secrets For Spinning Good Ideas Into Great Ideas

A Writer's Pocket Notebook

10 Secrets For Spinning Good Ideas Into Great Ideas

A Writer's Pocket Notebook

10 Secrets For Spinning Good Ideas Into Great Ideas

A Writer's Pocket Notebook

10 Secrets For Spinning Good Ideas Into Great Ideas

"Those Who Tell Their Stories Rule Society." **PLATO**

WRITERS RUN THE WORLD

APPENDIX
10 Secrets For Spinning Good Ideas Into Great Ideas

"You Can Trust Me with Everything, Except Your Pen!"

Sharon Esther Lampert

10 Secrets For Spinning Good Ideas Into Great Ideas

#1 Writer's Toolbox
BRAINSTORM FOR GREAT IDEAS
63

#2 Writer's Toolbox
ASK GREAT QUESTIONS
65

#3 Writer's Toolbox
TAKE GREAT NOTES
67

#4 Writer's Toolbox
GREAT OUTLINES AND ORGANIZATION
71

#5 Writer's Toolbox
GREAT RESEARCH: PRIMARY SOURCES
73

#6 Writer's Toolbox
GREAT CRITICAL THINKING TACTICS
75

#7 Writer's Toolbox
**10 ESOTERIC LAWS OF GENIUS AND CREATIVITY
BY PRODIGY SHARON ESTHER LAMPERT**
77

#8 Writer's Toolbox
READ GREAT WRITERS
79

#9 Writer's Toolbox
PROOFREADING TO PERFECTION
85

#10 Writer's Toolbox
FEEDBACK: FRESH EYES
87

"I can't understand why people are frightened of new ideas. I'm frightened of the old ones."
- John Cage

10 Secrets For Spinning Good Ideas Into Great Ideas

#1 Writer's Toolbox
BRAINSTORM FOR GREAT IDEAS

Step 1. Brainstorm for Great Ideas

    a. Generate a list of topics of interest.

    b. General Topics & Specific Topics

        * Politics: Presidential Elections

        * Travel: Florida Beaches and Sunscreens

        * Parenting: Reward vs. Punishment

        * Technology: GPS Is What Exactly?

Step 2. Good & Great Ideas

    a. Separate ideas into good & great ideas.

Good Ideas:	Great Ideas:
1.	1.
2.	2.
3.	3.
4.	4.
5.	5.
6.	6.
7.	7.
8.	8.
9.	9.
10.	10.

 **WRITERS RUN THE WORLD**

"If you would not be forgotten as soon as you are dead and rotten, either write something worth reading or do something worth writing."

—Benjamin Franklin

10 Secrets For Spinning Good Ideas Into Great Ideas

#2 Writer's Toolbox
Ask Great Questions
Who, What, Where, When, Why

The best way to acquire writing material is to ask questions.

Writing Exercise: Describe a Car

1. Ask Primary General Questions: Who? What? Where? When? Why?

    Q. Who owns the car?

    Q. What is the make and model of the car?

    Q. Where is the car kept?

    Q. When did you buy the car?

    Q. Why did you buy this car?

2. Ask Secondary Questions for Particular Details

    a. Is the car new or preowned?

    b. Are there any dents?

    c. How many repairs? Do you have repair documentation?

    d. Is the driver a man or a woman

    e. How big or small is the truck?

    f. Where is the car kept in inclement weather?

    g. Is the car used for the daily grind or for weekend pleasure?

 **WRITERS RUN THE WORLD**

"I can shake off
Everything if I write;
My sorrows disappear
My courage is reborn.

But, and that is the greatest question,
will I ever be able to write anything great,
will I ever become a journalist or a writer?
I hope so, oh, I hope so very much, for
I can recapture everything
when I write, my thoughts,
my ideas and my fantasies."

Anne Frank

10 Secrets For Spinning Good Ideas Into Great Ideas

#3 Writer's Toolbox
TAKE GREAT NOTES

1. Keep your notebook with you at all times.

2. Be ready to jot down any idea: bad, good or great.

3. Get into the habit of carrying your notebook and digital recorder everywhere you go.

4. If something captures your attention and you are in a public place, get out your book and write things down.

5. Use a pencil and eraser, so that you can read and revise.

6. Use this writing journal to record your ideas for stories, interviews, poems, song lyrics, movie scripts, recipes, etc.
    * Stories
    * Memories
    * Ideas
    * Interviews
    * Dialogue
    * Discoveries
    * Poem
    * Song Lyrics
    * Recipes

7. You also need a dictionary, thesaurus & guide for grammar usage?

WRITERS RUN THE WORLD

"No Fakes.
No Fat.
No Fluff.
No Filler.
No Flops.
No Flab.
No F-Bomb."
SEL

10 Secrets For Spinning Good Ideas Into Great Ideas

The Fine Line Between **GENIUS** and **INSANITY** Is **ORGANIZATION**

Sharon Esther Lampert
Poet, Philosopher, Prophet, Peacemaker & Prodigy

WRITERS RUN THE WORLD

#4 Writer's Toolbox
GREAT ORGANIZATION
Research, Lists, Ideas, Memories, Dialogue

Create A-Z Collections of Ideas, Topics and Lists:

C   * Characters
I   * Inspiration

      Fiction Writer:
      * Imagination, Free Association, Creativity

      Newspaper and Magazine Writer:
      * Interview Questions and Answers

D   * Dialogue

      * Discoveries

      Non-Fiction Writer:
F   * Research, Facts, Citations, and Critical Thinking
L   * Lists

      Memoir Writer:
M   * Memories
N   * New Vocabulary Words
P   * Poems
R   * Recipes
      * Reflections

S   * Song Lyrics

10 Secrets For Spinning Good Ideas Into Great Ideas

#4 Writer's Toolbox
GREAT ORGANIZATION
USE OUTLINES

1. Use Outlines to Focus Your Notes

    1. Netflix Shows
        a. Movies
        b. Documentaries
        c. Sports
        d. Cartooons

2. Underneath Every Idea, Write a Summary
Summaries help you focus on pinpointing your point of view.

3. Build a list of "Paragraphs" (3 paragraphs per page)

    Paragraph 1.
    Main Idea and Minor Ideas
        Supporting Examples
            Quotes
                Transition Words

    Paragraph 2.
    Main Idea and Minor Ideas
        Supporting Examples, Sources and Citations
            Direct or Indirect Quotes
                Transition Words to Unify Ideas

    Paragraph 3.
    Main Idea and Minor Ideas
        Supporting Examples, Sources, and Citations
            Direct or Indirect Quotes
                Transition Words to Unify Ideas

 **WRITERS RUN THE WORLD**

"My goal is to make sure every young person has the literacy skills they need to raise their voice and change their communities. That passion drives me every day!"
—Poet Amanda Gorman

10 Secrets For Spinning Good Ideas Into Great Ideas

#4 Writer's Toolbox
GREAT RESEARCH

Step 1. Use an Encyclopedia
Use the Encyclopedia to get a comprehensive overview of your subject matter. Who are the experts in the field?

Expert 1. _____

Expert 2. _____

Expert 3. _____

Step 2. Bibliographic Notes
Read the bibliographic notes for a list of the primary sources (autobiographical), and secondary sources (biographical, magazine and newspaper articles).

A. Primary Source: _____

B. Secondary Source: _____

Step 3. Pro and Con Arguments
Read the primary source materials for pro and con arguments.

A. Pro Argument: _____

B. Con Argument: _____

Step 4. Quotes
Read the primary source materials for direct and indirect quotes.

A. Direct Quote: _____

B. Indirect Quotes: _____

# WRITERS RUN THE WORLD

"I need solitude for my writing; not like a hermit – that wouldn't be enough… but like a dead man."
—Franz Kafka

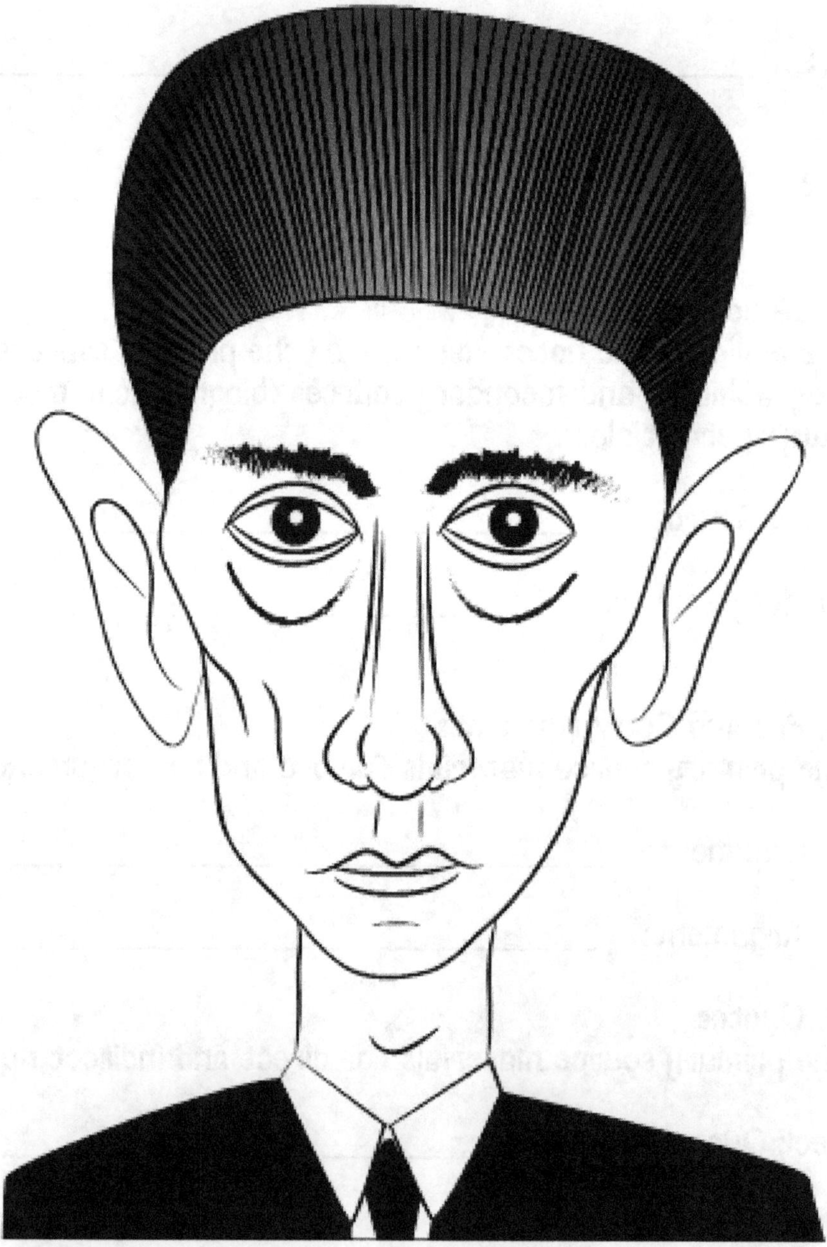

10 Secrets For Spinning Good Ideas Into Great Ideas

#6 Writer's Toolbox
GREAT CRITICAL THINKING TACTICS

*"BEWARE OF FALSE KNOWLEDGE;
IT IS MORE DANGEROUS THAN IGNORANCE."*
GEORGE BERNARD SHAW

1. **Keep an Open Mind**
   a. Weigh all sides of every question
   b. Prepare to probe the issue to the heart

2. **Use a Critical Mind**
   a. Separate facts from opinions

3. **Evaluate the Underlying Assumptions**
   a. Assumptions are a set of belief systems that are considered to be self-evident

4. **Use Inductive and Deductive Reasoning**
   a. Induction: Specific to General
   b. Deduction: General to Specific

5. **Evaluate Arguments Based on Fallacies:**
   a. Misdirected Appeals: e.g., Authority Popular Beliefs, Common Practice

   b. Emotional Appeals: e.g., Scare Tactics, Loyalty, Peer Pressure, Sob Story, Prejudice, Stereotypes, Hatred

WRITERS RUN THE WORLD

10 Esoteric Laws of Genius & Creativity
By Sharon Esther Lampert
Poet, Philosopher, Prophet, Peacemaker, Pinup, Prodigy

10 Secrets For Spinning Good Ideas Into Great Ideas

#7 Writer's Toolbox

Read My Book
Unleash The Creator, The GOD Within
10 Esoteric Laws of Genius & Creativity
by Sharon Esther Lampert

Part 1.
The Artist and Artwork Become One
1st Esoteric Law of Creativity
V.E.S.S.E.L.

2nd Esoteric Law of Creativity
INSPIRATION

3rd Esoteric Law of Creativity
IMPREGNATION

4th Esoteric Law of Creativity
INCUBATION

Part 2.
The Artist and Artwork Become Two
5th Esoteric Law of Creativity
GENESIS

The Artist
6th Esoteric Law of Creativity
SILENT:LISTEN

The Artwork
7th Esoteric Law of Creativity
METAMORPHOSIS

Part 3.
The Artist Mortal: The Artwork Immortal
8th Esoteric Law of Creativity
REVELATION

9th Esoteric Law of Creativity
SIGNATURE

10th Esoteric Law of Creativity
IMMORTALITY

WRITERS RUN THE WORLD

"If there is a book that you want to read, but it hasn't been written yet, you must be the one to write it!"
—Toni Morrison

10 Secrets For Spinning Good Ideas Into Great Ideas

#8 Writer's Toolbox
READ GREAT WRITERS

1. ### When You're not Writing—You're Reading!

2. ### Keep Up with the Newest Book Releases
   Sign up at your local library for the newsletter on the latest book releases. Download library apps into your cellephone. You can ready books, magazines and newspapers.

3. ### Something Over Nothing
   Even if you can't find the time to read the entire book, at least read a chapter or two to get a taste of the author's writing style. I pick up the lastest and greatest books at my local library, I read them in my favorite corner by the window sill with the natural light shining through. I spend 2 hours reading the books, and then return the books, because I don't have time to read the entirety of the books.

4. ### Join a Book of the Month Club
   Sometimes, it's best to read a chapter or two a week, and spread out the book over a few months.

5. ### Book Apps on Cell Phone
   Download books apps into your cell phone. I love them! The latest & greatest books are condensed into bullet points.

6. ### Bathroom Readers
   I have never taken reading material into the bathroom. I do have friends that do entertain themselves with books while frequenting the bathroom a few times a day. This is the something over nothing approach.

7. ### Public Transporation Readers
   Having lived in NYC for 20 years, most people riding the NYC subways are readers of newspapers, magazines and books.

WRITERS RUN THE WORLD

Read Great Writers

Title: _____

Author: _____

Title: _____

Author: _____

Title: _____

Author: _____

Title: _____

Author: _____

Title: _____

Author: _____

Title: _____

Author: _____

10 Secrets For Spinning Good Ideas Into Great Ideas

Read Great Writers

Title: __Unleash The Creator The God Within__
       __10 Esoteric Laws of Genius and Creativity__

Author: __Sharon Esther Lampert__

Title: __I Stole All the Words from the Dictionary__

Author: __Sharon Esther Lampert__

Title: _____

Author: _____

Title: _____

Author: _____

Title: _____

Author: _____

Title: _____

Author: _____

WRITERS RUN THE WORLD

Read Great Books

Title: _____

Author: _____

Title: _____

Author: _____

Title: _____

Author: _____

Title: _____

Author: _____

Title: _____

Author: _____

Title: _____

Author: _____

10 Secrets For Spinning Good Ideas Into Great Ideas

Read Great Books

Title: _____

Author: _____

Title: _____

Author: _____

Title: _____

Author: _____

Title: _____

Author: _____

Title: _____

Author: _____

Title: _____

Author: _____

WRITERS RUN THE WORLD

"Ever feel like this?

I'm exhausted!
I spent all morning putting in a comma and all afternoon taking it out!"
—Oscar Wilde

10 Secrets For Spinning Good Ideas Into Great Ideas

#9 Writer's Toolbox
PROOFREADING TO PERFECTION

"WRITING IS REWRITING."
- ROBERT L. KELLEY

1. Use Linear Left Brain and Proceed at a Turtle's Pace
2. Time and Tremendous Patience
3. Enlarge Text to 18+ Points
4. Read Aloud with TextEdit Speech Software

Proofread for Content:
1. Check Outline: Main Idea and Supporting Arguments
2. Check Research Materials for Primary Sources
3. Check Organization of Ideas
4. Check Redundancy
5. Check Paraphrasing – Avoid Careless Plagiarizing
6. Check Direct and Indirect Quotes
7. Check Word Choices
8. Check Cliches

"The conscious mind is the editor, and the subconscious mind is the writer. And the joy of writing, when you're writing from your subconscious, is beautiful – it's thrilling. When you're editing, which is your conscious mind, it's like torture."
— Steve Martin

Proofread for Structure:
1. Check Spelling
2. Check Grammar
3. Check Punctuation
4. Check Paragraph Format
5. Check Transition Words Between Ideas
   e.g., First, Second, Third, On one hand, On the other hand
6. Check Sentences
7. Check Wordiness
8. Check Agreement of Singular and Plural
9. Check Neatness

WRITERS RUN THE WORLD

PLEASE DON'T LET ME DIE WITH A TYPO!

Sharon Esther Lampert

Last Will & Testament

@2021. All Rights Reserved. WritersRunTheWorld.com

10 Secrets For Spinning Good Ideas Into Great Ideas

#10 Writer's Toolbox
Feedback: Fresh Eyes
5C: Comments, Corrections, Criticisms, Compliments and Citations

Join a writer's group where you will be able to hand out to each member of the group your written work, and ask for feedback from fresh eyes.

If you are still in touch with teachers from high school and college, you may also ask them to proofread your written work in exchange for cash or a gift card to a favorite restaurant.

Of course, there are many online editing services who will proofread your work for a nominal fee.

Whichever direction you decide to go, you must keep an **OPEN MIND** when criticisms as well as compliments are received.

Practice saying, "Thank you for your comments, corrections, compliments, and criticisms" even if your **EGO** is wounded in the exchange. Treat yourself to an ice cream cone to mend your wound.

Even if you read your manuscript 25 times, expect a **TYPO** to be overlooked. It really takes a pair of **FRESH EYES** to find irrational errors. Irrational errors are errors that have no rhyme or reason, yet have infiltrated your literary masterpiece.

One example of this type of error comes to mind with a 600+ page book I wrote. After publication, I accidentally came across one sentence that did not end with a period. So one sentence in a 600+ book has a missing period. Irritating to say the least! It's a completely irrational error! No rhyme! No reason!

Fortunately in the digital age, I was able to open the digital file, add the missing period, and republish my book.

Better yet, leave your manuscript **ALONE** for a month or two after its completion. After a brief hiatus, you will be able to see your own work with **FRESH EYES,** and make meaningful additions, subtractions, and corrections to your own work.

Years down the road, it is not an uncommon experience for a writer to no longer defend the same point of view that was vehemently argued in an article. To avoid present and future discreditation, find 5-10 pairs of **FRESH EYES** to address the **5Cs**. Include a copy of the **5C** form with a copy of your writing. Never give out the original!

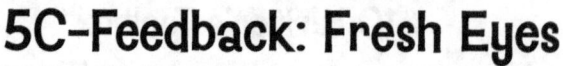

WRITERS RUN THE WORLD

5C-Feedback: Fresh Eyes

1. Comments
_____
_____
_____
_____

2. Corrections
_____
_____
_____
_____

3. Criticisms
_____
_____

4. Compliments
_____
_____

5. Citations
_____
_____

10 Secrets For Spinning Good Ideas Into Great Ideas

5C-Feedback: Fresh Eyes

1. Comments

_____

_____

_____

_____

2. Corrections

_____

_____

_____

3. Criticisms

_____

_____

4. Compliments

_____

_____

5. Citations

_____

_____

WRITERS RUN THE WORLD

Prodigy
Poet
Prophet
Philosopher
Peacemaker
Paladin of Education
Photon Superhero
Princess Kadimah 8TH
Pin-Up
Performer:Vocalist
Player:Jock
President
Publisher
Producer
Psychobiologist
Piano-Playing Cat
Polyglot
Phoenix

- SharonEstherLampert.com
- WorldFamousPoems.com
- PoetryJewels.com
- PhilosopherQueen.com
- PoetryEssentialService.com
- PhotonSuperHero.com
- Smartgrades.com
- EveryDayAnEasyA.com
- BooksNotBombs.com
- Schmaltzy.com
- TrueLoveBurnsEternal.com
- GodofWhat.com
- SillyLittleBoys.com
- 10Miracles.com
- PalmBeachBookPublisher.com
- WritersRunTheWorld.com
- PlannerParExcellence.com
- FloridaRetirementPlanner.com
- WorldPeaceEquation.com
- ArtHeart.store

FAN MAIL
FANS@sharonestherlampert.com

10 Secrets For Spinning Good Ideas Into Great Ideas

SHARON ESTHER LAMPERT
V.E.S.S.E.L. Very. Extra. Special. Sharon. Esther. Lampert.

POET
The Greatest Poems Ever Written on Extraordinary World Events

PROPHET
22 Commandments: All You Will Ever Need to Know About God
GOD TALKS TO ME: A Working Definition of God

Sharon's Mind Conceptualizes **BIG IDEAS** Using One Letter of the Alphabet

PHILOSOPHER
God of What? Is Life a Gift or a Punishment?
Temporary Insanity 13 — **Written in Letter S**
The Sperm Manifesto: 10 Rules for the Road

PEACEMAKER
World Peace Equation
www.worldpeaceequation.com

PRODIGY
- UNLEASH THE CREATOR THE GOD WITHIN
  10 Esoteric Laws of Genius and Creativity
- CUPID — **Written in Letter C**
- AMNON: Hidden World of Sex, Art and Genius
- In 5 Minutes, Learn 5000 Years of Jewish History
- DESTINY: Life By Default or Design? — **Written in Letter D**
- The Secret Sauce of Book Sales — **Written in Letter P**
- Silly Little Boys: 40 Rules of Manhood, www.sillylittleboys.com

PALADIN OF EDUCATION
The Silent Crisis Destroying America's Brightest Minds
BOOK OF THE MONTH, ALMA PUBLIC LIBRARY
- 40 Universal Gold Standards of Education
- 10 SMARTGRADES Ace Every Test Every Time
- 15 Stepping Stones of Academic Success
- 15 Stumbling Blocks of Academic Failure
  www.Smartgrades.com

PHOTON SUPERHERO OF EDUCATION
www.PhotonSuperhero.com

PIN-UPS
SEXIEST CREATIVE GENIUS IN HUMAN HISTORY

PERFORMER
Vocalist: Ashira Orchestra (YouTube Videos)

WRITERS RUN THE WORLD

My Favorite Quotes on Writing

"It is perfectly okay to write garbage —
as long as you edit brilliantly."
— C. J. Cherryh

"Write drunk, edit sober."
— Ernest Hemingway

"The letter I have written today is longer than usual
because I lacked the time to make it shorter."
– Blaise Pascal (1623-1662)

"The original writer is not he
who refrains from imitating others,
but he who can be imitated by none."
– Francois Rene de Chateaubriand (1768-1848)

"The difference between fiction and reality?
Fiction has got to make sense."
– Tom Clancy (b. 1947)

"Copy from one, it's plagiarism;
copy from two, it's research."
– Wilson Mizner (1876-1933)

"The artist is nothing without the gift,
but the gift is nothing without work."
– Emile Zola (1840-1902)

"Don't tell me the moon is shining;
show me the glint of light on broken glass."
– Anton Chekhov (1860-1904)

"One should not aim at being possible to understand,
but at being impossible to misunderstand."
– Quintilian (Marcus Fabius Quintilianus, 1st century AD)

"You don't write because you want to say something,
you write because you have something to say."
– F. Scott Fitzgerald (1896-1940)

10 Secrets For Spinning Good Ideas Into Great Ideas

My Favorite Movies on Writers

#1st Favorite - Genius: Life of Editor Max Perkins (2016)

#2nd Favorite - Promise at Dawn (2017)

The Man Who Knew Infinity (2015)

Toni Morrison: The Pieces I Am (2019)

EXCELLENT! DON'T MISS!
Genius Series By Bettany Hughes (2016)
Genius of The Ancient World
Buddha, Socrates, and Confucius
Genius of the Modern World
Karl Marx, Frederick Nietzsche, and Sigmund Freud

MANK (2020)

Joan Didion: The Center Will Not Hold (2017)

Mary Shelley (2017)

The Wife (2017)

Colette (2018)

Hannah Arendt (2013)

The Words (2012)

The Pen Is Mightier Than the Sword
Edward Bulwer-Lytton, 1839

Sara Blakely  • Following
Founder and CEO of SPANX
1d • 🌐

A glimpse into my notebook collection. Every year since the start of @spanx, I've had a notebook with me. It's the same kind, same size, from the drug store. I have shelves and shelves of them full of ideas, goals, thoughts, sketches, people I've met, and my appointments. If I don't have a notebook with me, I feel lost. I've heard it said... "If you have a goal write it down. If you do not write it down, you do not have a goal- you have a wish." Write it down!

 **Carol Duhart** • 3rd+   1d (edited) •••
Marketing and Communications Ma...

And I was just throwing my notebooks away. I'm totally keeping them now. I'm calling them the "Days of Future Past."

Fair Use Legal Disclaimer
Copyright Disclaimer under Section 107 of the copyright act 1976, allowance is made for fair use for purposes such as criticism, comment, news reporting, scholarship, and research. Fair use is a use permitted by copyright statute that might otherwise be infringing. Non-profit, educational or personal use tips the balance in favour of fair use."

www.ingramcontent.com/pod-product-compliance
Lightning Source LLC
Chambersburg PA
CBHW081353080526
44588CB00016B/2478